About this Book

Would you know where to look for a plant to cure a cough, which to choose to cure a stomachache, or to polish a pot? The early settlers knew. They depended upon many of the plants we think of as weeds today for food and medicine.

This book tells about some of those plants. It describes where they came from and what they were used for. It tells how you can learn a great deal about each plant from its Latin name and why some common names are misleading.

To help you to find the plant out-of-doors, the plants are grouped in three sections—those growing in the woods, those found in pastures, and those in swampland. The plants in each of these three general habitats are grouped again according to the uses the pioneers made of them.

A large, accurate illustration of each plant accompanies its description. Included are directions on how to start your own herb garden, collecting and drying plants, making teas and salads, dyeing cloth, and an index.

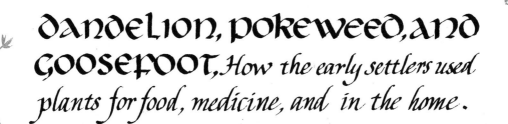

DANDELION, POKEWEED, AND GOOSEFOOT. *How the early settlers used plants for food, medicine, and in the home.*

By Elizabeth Schaeffer

With Illustrations by Grambs Miller

Young Scott Books

Text Copyright © 1972 by Elizabeth Schaeffer
Illustrations Copyright © 1972 by Grambs Miller
All Rights Reserved
Young Scott Books
Addison-Wesley Publishing Company, Inc.
Reading, Massachusetts 01867
Printed in the United States of America
Second Printing

GO/BP   09304   10/73

Library of Congress Cataloging in Publication Data
Schaeffer, Elizabeth, 1939-
Dandelion, pokeweed, and goosefoot.
SUMMARY: Describes the various plants used by the
early settlers as food and medicine and includes recipes
as well as instructions for starting a herb garden.
1. Botany, Economic—U. S.—Juvenile literature.
[1. Botany, Economic.   2. Folk medicine.   3. Food]
I. Miller, Grambs, illus.   II. Title.
SB108.U5S3   581.6'1'0973   72-1836
ISBN 0-201-09304-9

Contents

PART I

Old Plants and New
An International Code
What Is an Herb?

Old Plants and New

The early settlers came to America to find freedom, or adventure, or a new way of life. Most of them found all three. When they arrived, however, they needed something even more basic—food and shelter. The settlers had brought some food with them from their homes in Europe, but most of it was used in the long sea voyage. A good crossing could take a month. When the small wooden sailing ships met storms or bad winds, the voyage took much, much longer. The settlers brought seeds and roots of the plants they had used for food in their homelands, but they could not be sure the seeds and roots would grow in this new land. Often, the ships landed in the New World so late in the year that crops did not have time to grow before a killing frost in the fall. In many places, forests had to be cleared before seeds could be planted. Until the following year, when crops could be planted, the settlers had only the native wild plants the friendly Indians showed them how to use as food.

In the following years, fields were cleared, the ground tilled, and the seeds planted. Some of the seeds from Europe grew well in the rich, newly tilled soil of the forest clearings. Others grew poorly or not at all. Some did so well that now we see them everywhere in the United States and we think of them as weeds. On the other hand, the settlers liked some of the native plants so much that they planted them in their gardens alongside the European newcomers.

As the pioneers moved west, they did not have time to stay in one place long enough to plant a new crop and wait for the harvest. Once again, they relied on the little food they could take, and, most of all, on the wild plants they learned about from the Indians.

Some of the plants you can find in North America now were neither native nor brought for a purpose by the settlers. They were the hitchhikers. The hitchhikers spread most rapidly because of their ways of distributing their seeds. If a seed survived the trip across the Atlantic without any care, it would spread with relative ease on land. Seeds crossed the Atlantic in shoes, on the hems of long skirts, and in the bags of other seeds to be used in the settlers' new gardens. Many of them were brought in the ballast of ships. In colonial days, ships leaving the ports of Europe to bring back goods from the new land took on soil dug from waste places near the docks to use as ballast. When a ship reached port in the colonies, the sailors dumped the soil ballast overboard to make room for the valuable cargo. The soil contained many seeds which found a good place to grow and start new plants in the New World.

One story to illustrate how new plants came to North America as hitchhikers tells about a small factory on the banks of the Naugatuck River near Waterbury, Connecticut. The company had sent to Europe for old rubber boots that they could melt down to make new rubber things needed in this country. The factory workers then took the old cloth liners out of the boots and piled the liners up to burn. The river flooded before the pile could be burned, and the flood waters carried the liners, and the seeds that had been caught in them when they were worn in Europe, down the river and left them in the soft mud of the river bank. The mud was an ideal place for the seeds to grow, and soon many new flowers were blooming on the banks of the Naugatuck River that had not grown there before. It took the detective work of a botanist years later to solve the mystery of how they got there.

Many of the wild plants in this book are found only in the eastern half of the United States. This is so for several reasons. First, the plants that came over from Europe grew on the eastern coast and spread from there. Second, the environment for growing, or biome, is much the same over the eastern half of North America. The word biome means a combination of sun, water, soil, and all the other things that affect the life of a plant or animal. Very simply, biome means home. The biome of the eastern half of North America was made up of forest land with shade and plentiful moisture for plants. This means that plants that grow well in shade and moist soil grow well in the eastern half of the country. Originally, this eastern forest extended into Illinois and Wisconsin where it met the great central prairie. The biome of the prairie is based on ample sun and at least some time of dry soil each year. Naturally, the many plants that had adapted well to the forest biome stopped at the line between the forest and the prairie. The Rocky Mountains made another barrier. The means of seed dispersal—

wind and animals—both were stopped by the steep Rampart Range of the eastern Rockies.

Within these two large general biomes there are many smaller variations. In this book, we will talk about two of these smaller, more special kinds of plant homes. One of these is the swamp. You can find swamps in both the forest and the prairie biomes, wherever there is ground that stays wet all year. Usually these swamps are sunny, simply because few trees can grow where the ground stays wet. Certain plants can grow here in the swamp that cannot grow anywhere else.

The other special kind of plant home is the city. Plants from all three of the other kinds of homes can find a place to grow in the city if they find soil, sun, and water. It is harder for a plant to grow in the city because of the pollutants that are often in the air, and because the rich topsoil has been bulldozed away to make room for foundations for the buildings. If a plant is tolerant of this environment, though, it often finds an advantage in the city that its country relatives do not have. The warmth of the sun is caught by the walls of the buildings, giving the city plant a longer growing season. Often you can see plants green and growing by the south wall of a building in very early spring when the countryside is still brown and dry. If you cannot go to the country to see the plants in this book, look in the vacant lots and alleys where you live. You might find sour grass, dock, dandelion, mullein, purslane, goosefoot, chicory, and yarrow—and even more, if you look carefully.

Many of the wildflowers we call weeds—both those brought from Europe and the native ones—are weeds of cultivation. This means two things. First, these weeds will grow wherever the ground is plowed, even in a city. They are not dependent on a natural biome to grow, but follow wherever man goes. If a field is left long enough, the native plants will eventually return with the return of the native trees. This takes a long time. Many times, a piece of ground is cleared and then left only partly cultivated to make a road or a pasture. These roadsides and pastures make good growing places for weeds of cultivation. Secondly, these weeds of cultivation are the plants we often like the least because they grow unasked-for in gardens where we want other kinds of plants to grow.

An International Code

In this book we will use the Latin names of the plants as well as the common names. These Latin names are an international code anyone can use when he wants to be sure people will know exactly the plant he is talking about. The Latin name is the same for the same plant all over the world. Some widely spread plants can have dozens of common, or folk, names, each used by people living in different locations within the total growing area of the plant. On the other hand, two or three plants may be called by the same name by different people. The marigold mentioned in the herbals of the early settlers as a good food and flavorful in soups is what most of us now call *calendula.* The flower most of us think of as a marigold is the French or African marigold. The swamp or marsh marigold is another flower altogether. Without the Latin names to help us, talking about marigolds could be confusing.

Another reason for the Latin code is that if you know the meaning of the code, you can learn a good deal about the plant. Latin names, like common ones, are given for a reason. Sometimes the name will tell you what the plant is used for. *Lavandula,* the Latin name for lavender, means something to wash with—as in our word "lavatory." A long time ago, lavender was used to perfume the water and soap to wash with. *Esculentus* means edible—a food plant. *Medicus* means medicine—a plant used to cure illness. *Officinalis* is more specific, and means that the plant it describes was an official cure for something. *Pulmonaria* is still more specific, and means a plant that contains a medicine to cure illnesses of the lungs. The Latin word for lung is *pulmo*.

Many plants were called by the names of parts of the body. This was done according to an old belief called the doctrine of signatures. People who believed in the doctrine of signatures thought that you could tell what illnesses a plant could cure by looking at the shape of the flowers, leaves, and roots. For instance, *pulmonaria* would be good for the lungs because its leaves were shaped like lungs. *Hepatica* has leaves both the shape and color of the liver—therefore it was thought to be good medicine for the liver. The name they gave the plant, *hepatica,* comes from the Latin name for liver. The walnut was one of the best medicines for illnesses of the head, according to the doctrine of signatures. The outer husk looked like the head. The shell inside the husk looked like the skull. And finally, the nut inside the shell looked like the brain. For this reason, walnut husks were used to rub on the head. One of the things this was supposed to do was turn grey hair brown again. Since the husks of walnuts have a brown dye in them, it just happened to work! Not all of the plants named by the doctrine of signatures were that helpful.

In the years when this country was being explored and its native flowers named, the doctrine of signatures was an important theory in medicine. You can see this not only in the Latin names, but in the common names the early settlers called the plants around them—pleurisy root, lung-wort, liverwort, and throatwort. Often, they simply combined the name of the part of the body the plant was supposed to heal with the word "wort," the ancient English word for plant.

Latin names can tell us where a plant grows. Most of the states of the United States have a flower named for them because it was first seen in that state. You can find names like *virginiana, californica, marilandica,* and so on. In the English common names, we have Virginia bluebell and California poppy. These names can trick you, though, unless you know a little history. When many of our native wild-flowers were being named, the French owned much of North America west of the Mississippi. This land was called Louisiana. Later, when this land was owned by the United States, much of this area was called the Missouri Territory. Flowers found there were often named *louisianus* and *missouriensis,* even though they were not growing anywhere near the present states of Louisiana and Missouri.

The kind of land the plant grows on is another piece of information you can find in Latin names. *Rivularis* means stream-loving. *Montanus* means of the mountains. *Maritimus* means by the sea. The common names tell us where the plants grow, too. You can find prairie evening primrose, mountain aster, and roadside thistle.

Many times the Latin name describes the plant. You can see the English word in *cavus*—hollow, *curvatus*—curved, and *equalis*—equal. All these words are used to describe some part of a plant. The colors of a flower are often used to help identify the plant. *Roseus* means rose-colored. *Purpureus* means purple. *Albidus* means white, like the word "albino." *Luteus* means yellow. *Coelestis* means blue. The common names of the plants goldenrod, bluebells, scarlet paintbrush, prickly poppy, and clammy ground cherry all tell us much about the appearance of the plants.

Finally, many Latin names were taken from the names of people that the discoverer of the plant wanted to honor. We have *washingtonia* for George Washington, *franklinia* for Ben Franklin, and even *lewisia* and *clarkia* for Lewis and Clark. Often the name was the name of a doctor. Since plants were one of the few sources of medicine in colonial times, most doctors were also botanists. Nicolas Monardes, a Spanish doctor who lived in the latter half of the sixteenth century, wrote one of our first books on the plants of North America. He was honored by having the *Monardas*—members of the mint family—named after him. Drs. Gaultier, Mitchell, and Menzies were all doctors who have had North American wildflowers named in their honor.

Some common names of the native wildflowers were given more to honor people of the Bible, and to honor (or tease) the settlers' own friends rather than to honor great and famous men. These names include St. John's wort, St. Peter's wort, and black-eyed Susan, sweet Betty, and stinking Willie.

What Is an Herb?

The settlers themselves would not have differentiated between food plants and healing herbs. Our word "vegetable" is more recent than the settling of this country. The pioneers called any plant that could be eaten an herb—carrots, beets, and lettuce included. "Herb" also meant any plant that could be used as medicine. There was no great difference between medicine and food in those days. The early settlers held to the practical thought that what was good for you was good for you whether you were well or ailing. Later on, when the plants came to be called vegetables, the name for them was taken from the Latin word, *vegetabilis,* which means life-giving.

The pioneers didn't know that the vitamins in green plants were often what they lacked, especially in winter. Many of the illnesses the settlers suffered from were not caused by bacteria or a virus, but by the lack of vitamin A or B or C or one of the many vitamins fresh green foods give us. Fresh greens were among the most common herbal cures given in the spring. The herbs given to "thin the blood"—the spring tonics—really did help because they supplied those missing vitamins. Even the unusual promise that some of these spring tonics would make loose teeth firm again has a basis in fact. Scurvy, a vitamin deficiency disease, can be cured by doses of vitamin C. One symptom of scurvy is weakening of the gums and loosening of the teeth. The Indians, too, ate greens and berries as a cure for scurvy, although they didn't understand the real reason why they worked so well.

Many types of tea made from green herbs were given to people sick with fever. Aside from any truly medicinal value each herb might have had, these herb teas were useful for several reasons. The liquid helped to reduce the fever, the small amount of sugar or honey gave the patient some energy, and the mild flavor helped to soothe a queasy stomach. Many of the herbs of the mint family were used to make these teas. Horehound, catnip, horse balm, sage, thyme, spearmint, peppermint, and hyssop were some of the mints the early settlers used to make healing teas.

Many of the herbs brought to this country for medicine are still being used in herb gardens, although now we use them for flavoring food. Chives, sage, mint, thyme, dill, and rue are some herbs you can still find in gardens, in seed catalogues, and in grocery stores.

Of course, many of the values of the herbs were exaggerated and some just didn't work. There is an old rhyme about *borage,* a kind of forget-me-not, that goes "I borage bring alwaies courage." We don't believe this any more, but then we still call the plant "forget-me-not" even when we don't believe it strengthens anyone's memory.

To understand about the plants used more specifically as medicine, we will need to use a few medical terms. Many of these you already know.

Antiseptic: a medicine to kill bacteria or germs.

Astringent: a mild styptic, used for its refreshing qualities externally as a lotion or internally as a tea.

Cathartic: a medicine given to "clean out the system." A strong laxative.

Diuretic: a medicine given to remove excess water from the body.

Germicide: a germ killer. *Cide* means to kill, so germicide is a germ killer. Bacteriacide means a killer of bacteria. Fungicide kills fungus.

Laxative: a medicine to relieve a stomachache by speeding up the process of elimination of whatever in the stomach or intestines is causing the stomachache.

Sedative: a medicine given to relax or to bring on sleep.

Styptic: a medicine applied outside the body, or externally, to stop bleeding.

The plants you will read about in this book are grouped so that you can locate them more easily. There are three general sections—woodland, pastureland, and swampland. Within each of these three sections, plants are grouped according to the uses made of them by the pioneers—as food, as medicine, and for household purposes.

All of the plants were important to the settlers' way of life. Perhaps after reading about them and locating them in your neighborhood, some of these plants might become useful to you, too.

PART II

Plants of the Woodland,
Pastureland, and Swampland

Plants of the Woodland

medicine

wintergreen *Gaultheria procumbens*

Dr. Gaultier of Quebec was one of the many doctors in early America who was interested in the native herbs and their uses in medicine. Wintergreen was officially named *gaultheria* in his honor. Oil of wintergreen is still used in many medicines to soothe stomachs and in many more to mask other less pleasant flavors. The next time you go to a drugstore, look along the shelves to see how many medicines include oil of wintergreen. This oil can be obtained from both the leaves and the berries by boiling the plant. It is interesting to know that oil of wintergreen can also be taken from the bark of a birch tree. Wintergreen, sometimes called teaberry or checkerberry, can be found in woods and clearings in the eastern half of the country. The white flowers bloom from June to September. The edible red berries follow soon after the flowers. Look for them near the ground. Wintergreen is only two to six inches tall.

GILL-OVER-THE-GROUND *Glechoma hederacea*

This creeping mint is now a very common weed. You can smell that it is a mint as you pull it out of your garden. Once, this herb was used by housewives both as a medicinal tea, and to brew beer. The "gill" of gill-over-the-ground is from the French word meaning to brew. The purple flowers bloom from April to July. Catnip is still another mint brought to this country from Europe for its medicinal value. For cats, it seems to be a stimulant. For people, a tea made from its leaves serves to soothe the nerves. The Latin name for catnip is *Nepeta cataria*.

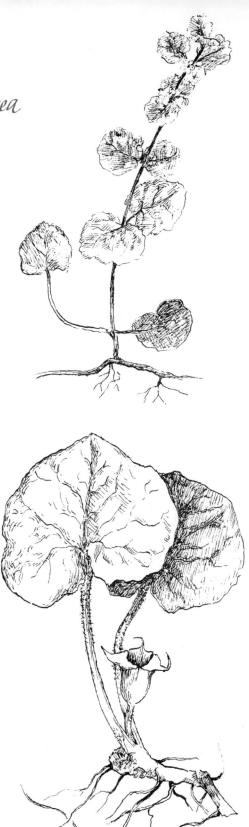

WILD GINGER *Asarum canadense*

This is one of the native herbs in North America that settlers used as a substitute for a spice they had been familiar with at home in Europe. The plant grows in shady wooded areas. You need to look closely to see the flowers, because they are so close to the ground. There is a reason for this. This plant is pollinated by a beetle that crawls into the flower. The root has the flavor of ginger, and was used both as a spice and as a cure for indigestion and whooping cough.

mint *Mentha*

Many mints were used as medicine in colonial times, as they are today. Any medicine you see with the ingredient "mentha" in it has some form of mint in it. *Mentha* simply means mint in Latin. Mint is often used now as it was in colonial days to soothe an upset stomach or a sore throat. There are two kinds of mint that are usually just called "mint." One is *Mentha spicata* — spearmint. The other is *Mentha piperita* — peppermint. Both of these mints have escaped from old gardens and can be found wild now in the eastern woodlands where the ground is moist. They share with the other members of the mint family the characteristic square stem. The combination of a minty smell and a square stem is a sure sign of one of the mints.

ευρατοπιυμ *Eupatorium purpureum*

Mithridates Eupator, King of Pontus around 120 B.C., gave his name to these autumn flowering plants when he discovered that they were a cure for a certain kind of poison. Later, in this country, another member of the *Eupatorium* family was called Joe-Pye-weed after Joe Pye, an Indian medicine man who used the plant to cure fevers. The settlers also used the plant to cure fevers and gave it the name of feverwort. Sometimes a member of this family is called boneset. This does not mean it was used to set bones, but that its dried leaves made a tea that cured a fever called bone-break fever because of the violent convulsions that came with it. Another member of this family, the white snakeroot, is deadly. It is the plant that poisoned the settlers' cows and gave the settlers who drank the milk the dreaded milk sickness. Nancy Hanks, Abraham Lincoln's mother was one of its victims. White snakeroot has white flowers, as the name tells you. Can you tell what color flowers *Eupatorium purpureum* has? Many plants of this family grow in wet woods from the Atlantic to the Rocky Mountains.

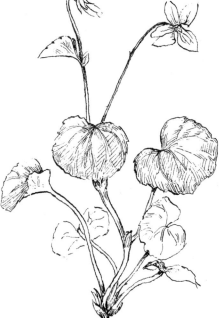

violets *Viola*

Violets were used, as were so many other plants, both as food and as medicine. Medicine to soothe the eyes was found in violets. The flowers were used to make a very pretty candy. Young violet leaves and the flowers can also be used in salads. Violets can be found all over Europe and North America. There are seventy-seven kinds of violets that are native to North America alone. You can find them blooming from April to June. Most of the flowers are violet color, but some violets are white and some are yellow.

may apple *Podophyllum peltatum*

This native of the open woodlands of eastern North America is a plant with many uses. The fruit, which looks something like a lemon and has a sharp lemon-like flavor when ripe, was used by the settlers as a substitute for lemons to flavor food. The Indians taught the settlers to boil the roots for a cathartic. This was very powerful medicine, however, and could kill if too much was taken. Two drugs taken from the root of *Podophyllum peltatum* are still being used. One, Podophyllin, is still used when a strong cathartic is needed. The other, a group of drugs called the peltatins, is being experimented with in the search for a cure for cancer. You can find the yellow and white flower under the umbrella-shaped leaf in the spring. If you want to try flavoring some food with the fruit, be very sure it is ripe. Even when it is ripe, the taste is very sharp.

COLTSFOOT *Tussilago farfara*

Coltsfoot has been naturalized over the eastern half of North America for a long time. This is a very old herb, and was one of the first to be brought here from Europe. The leaves were used by the ancient Greeks as candy and to make tea. *Tussilago* means cough-chaser, which tells us that the official use of the plant was to cure coughs. In medieval Europe, the coltsfoot was such a common medicine that apothecaries or druggists, painted pictures of the plant on the doors of their shops to show those who could not read where to buy drugs and medicines. Coltsfoot blooms in March and April and can be found in wet places and along brooks. The dandelion-like flowers come up long before the leaves appear in the spring.

SOUR GRASS *Oxalis stricta*

This herb is native both to Europe and to North America. The sour-tasting leaves are often eaten in salads and were once used as a remedy for a stomachache. Since the leaves are rich in oxalic acid, eating too many of them could bring on the stomachache they were supposed to cure. All summer you can find this herb blooming in woods, old cultivated places, and even in vacant lots in cities. The little flowers are bright yellow.

witch hazel, *Hamamelis virginiana*

Witch hazel is another of the settlers' herbs that you can find in a drugstore. The native kind of witch hazel, *Hamamelis virginiana* is considered the best for medicinal use. It is used today the way the settlers used it, as a soothing astringent lotion for insect bites and skin irritations. The Iroquois Indians made a medicinal astringent tea of the leaves. Witch hazel is a bush that grows in eastern North America. Its yellow flowers, looking like tassels, bloom very late in the fall.

feverfew *Parthenium integrifolium*

This plant was called wild quinine by the settlers. Both of the common names tell us that this plant was used to ease a fever. It is another example of a native plant that was pressed into service when the plant the settlers brought from Europe was not available. The European feverfew grows in sunny places, not in woodlands. It is the feverfew that you can find in gardens now. American feverfew grows in light woodlands in eastern North America where it blooms from July to September. The yellow and white flowers look like small daisies.

poison ivy *Rhus radicans*

"Leaflets three—let it be!
Berries red—never dread!"
Poison ivy is very variable in its growth. It may be a vine, a woody bush, or just a small sprig of a plant. The leaves may be as small as two inches or as large as ten or twelve inches. The leaflets are always in threes, though, so if you see them, do not touch! The flowers are very small and greenish-white and so are the berries—never red. The old rhyme is a good one to remember. Lacquerware is made from the sap of *Rhus verniciferum*—a relative of our *Rhus radicans*. Some people are so allergic to poison ivy that they cannot touch lacquerware without getting a rash. Another close relative is *Anacardium occidentale*. We know this one better as the cashew nut. Before they are roasted cashew nuts can give you *dermatitis,* or skin irritation, just like poison ivy. Poison ivy grows almost everywhere in North America. Moist shady ground seems to be its favorite place to grow, but it can be found in many other areas as well.

jewel weed *Impatiens pallida*

Fortunately, the jewel weed often grows near poison ivy, for it likes the same shady, moist ground. The juice of the jewel weed is an old folk remedy for poison ivy rash. The juice may merely dilute the poison and wash it off, but there is evidence that it acts against the poison in some way. The watery juice of the crushed stems of jewel weed is rubbed on the part of the body that touched the poison ivy. Jewel weed is found in the eastern half of North America where it blooms from July to September. The yellow blooms hang down from the branches like earrings. This gives the flower one of its folk names, ladies' ear-drops. Jewel weed is interesting for another reason, too. The pioneers called it "touch-me-not" and "quick-in-the-hand" because when the seeds are ripe, the seed pod explodes and shoots the seeds into the air. This gives the plant its Latin name *Impatiens,* meaning impatient.

food

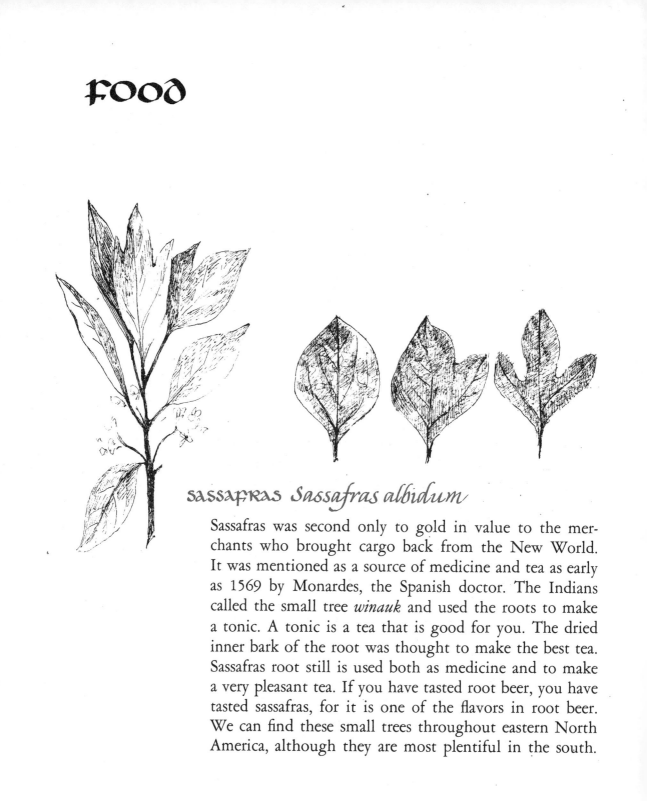

sassafras *Sassafras albidum*

Sassafras was second only to gold in value to the merchants who brought cargo back from the New World. It was mentioned as a source of medicine and tea as early as 1569 by Monardes, the Spanish doctor. The Indians called the small tree *winauk* and used the roots to make a tonic. A tonic is a tea that is good for you. The dried inner bark of the root was thought to make the best tea. Sassafras root still is used both as medicine and to make a very pleasant tea. If you have tasted root beer, you have tasted sassafras, for it is one of the flavors in root beer. We can find these small trees throughout eastern North America, although they are most plentiful in the south.

nettles *Urtica*

Urtica gracilis is the most common nettle in North America. It grows over much of northern North America. European nettles had long been used as food. When the early settlers came to America, they used the native *Urtica gracilis* the way they had used *Urtica pilulifera* and others in Europe. The settlers cooked nettle leaves as we cook spinach and used them in stews and soups. The fibers of the stems were used to make a linen-like cloth. To some early settlers, particularly those from Scotland, the nettle cloth was finer than the finest linen. Be careful of nettles! They have stinging hairs that can give you a very painful rash. Only the very young shoots of nettles are used as food—before the stinging hairs develop. In fact, *urticaria* is the medical term for a bad rash. The settlers used the sap of the dock plant to wash out the stinging poison of the nettles when they had brushed against the mature plants by accident.

Shadblow *Amelanchier canadensis*

This is a tree of the eastern half of North America. It is one of the first to bloom in the spring. In fact, it blooms when the shad, a species of fish, swim upstream to spawn. This gives it the folk name of shadblow. Blow is the old English word for bloom. The Indians ate the berries fresh and dried them for winter use. The settlers used them for pies and jams as well.

papaw *Asimina triloba*

This small tree bears a fruit which tastes like a pulpy banana. The Indians showed the early settlers that this fruit was good to eat. The settlers may have needed some reassurance before trying it, though, for the skin is a strange purple-brown and the smell is heavy and a little too sweet. You can find papaw in wooded areas in the southern states from the Atlantic to the central plains.

persimmon *Diospyros virginiana*

The Latin name for persimmon means "divine wheat to be found in the Virginias." "Divine" makes sense, for the fruits of this tree, when fully ripe, are delicious. *Virginiana* makes sense, for the tree was found in the Virginias of the early colonies. But why "wheat?" That will remain a mystery. While the fruit is good to eat when it is fully ripe, it is very, very sour until that time. Don't try to eat a persimmon that is not soft and orange-colored! Persimmons grow in the south usually, but a few grow as far north as Connecticut.

household

pokeweed *Phytolacca americana*

This tall purple-stemmed plant has been used to make food, medicine, dyes, and ink, as well. Our name "pokeweed" comes from the Algonquin Indian name, *pucoon,* meaning "plant with dye." Inkberry is another name for pokeweed. The early settlers used pokeweed berries to make ink to write their letters, dye to color their clothes, and even paint to paint pictures. In early spring, when the shoots are young and still green, the pioneers collected the pokeweed leaves to use as food. In some parts of the country even now, poke greens are a favorite spring food. After the purple dye develops in the stems and berries, however, the pokeweed contains a kind of poison. In very small doses this poison was used medicinally both by the Indians and by the settlers. Pokeweed is a very tall plant, growing from four to twelve feet high. It dies back to the ground each winter and sends up the green shoots each spring. You can find it in woods, roadsides, and even sometimes in city lots.

ELDERBERRY *Sambucus canadensis*

This tall bush, or small tree, provided something for each member of a pioneer family. The women used the berries to make pies and jam and wine. They made face lotions from the flowers, and dyes for their clothes from the berries. The men used the straight, finely grained wood of the stems to make smooth pegs and dowels, serving until a more permanent peg could be hand-carved of pine. The children pushed the soft pithy centers out of the smooth stems and used them to make flutes as the Indians had done. The boys used the same tubes to make excellent pea-shooters. The men used these hollow stems too, in the way that probably gave the elder its name. Elder comes from "aeld," the ancient Anglo-Saxon word for fire. These hollow stems were used to blow air into the center of a pile of kindling to help start a fire.

The flat, white clusters of bloom can be seen in June and July. The berries come in early fall. You can find elderberry along the edges of woods and streams anywhere in eastern North America. *Sambucus pubens* is very similar, except that it has red berries in a pointed cluster, while *Sambucus canadensis* has deep purple berries in a flat cluster.

Plants of the Pastureland

medicine

dandelion *Taraxacum officinale*

It is hard to believe, but no dandelion had bloomed in North America until the colonists brought dandelions with them for food and medicine. Remember the meaning of *officinalis?* The dandelion was once the official remedy for illness that came on in the winter. The same qualities in the plant that make it such a persistent pest now, made it a rich and much-needed source of vitamins for the early settlers. The dandelion stays green long into the winter and grows green again with the first warm sun of early spring. It can do this because of the food it stores in its deep taproot. The settlers used the greens as spring tonic and as a vegetable. They used the youngest leaves in salads and boiled the less tender ones. They roasted the roots to make a coffee-like drink. They even made wine from the blossoms! Now we see dandelions all over North America, even in the cities. The familiar yellow flowers come mostly in the spring, but you can usually see a few blooms all summer and into the fall.

GOLDENROD *Solidago*

There are more than 125 species of goldenrod, most of them native to North America. When the colonies were being settled, goldenrod was considered to be a very rare and useful herb. Great cargoes of it were taken to England where the dried leaves were sold to make medicine. The seeds of goldenrod are very viable, or easily grown, and soon goldenrod was growing in England, too. Can you see a word you know in *Solidago?* The medicine made from it was thought to make you solid, or well, again. Goldenrod is a very easy wildflower to find when it blooms in the fall. It grows in any dry, sunny place in the eastern half of North America. It is very hard to tell just which goldenrod you have found, though, once you have found it. The many kinds are all very much alike, and even trained botanists sometimes have trouble identifying them.

chamomile *Anthemis cotula*

Anthemis cotula has many folk names—white stinkweed, stinking daisy, and pig-sty daisy. You can guess that it has a very unpleasant smell. Its European relative, *Anthemis nobilis,* was brought to this country because of its usefulness as a tea for upset stomach and for fever. *Anthemis nobilis,* or noble Anthemis, has a very pleasant smell. Because of this, it is used even today as an ingredient in hair rinses. No one would want to use pig-sty daisy that way. The two chamomiles look very much alike. Both look like small daisies with fernlike leaves. It is easy to tell which one you have found by the smell. They grow in areas of old cultivation where they bloom all summer.

HORSEMINT *Monarda punctata*

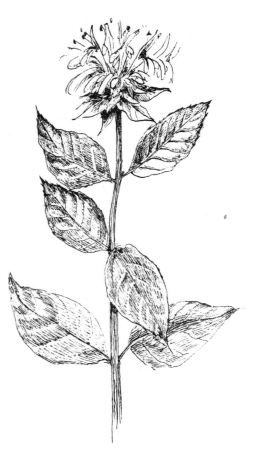

Horsemint and Oswego tea, *Monarda didyma* were both used to make medicinal teas. They are very much alike, except horsemint has light purple flowers and Oswego tea has red ones. Horsemint actually has nothing to do with horses. "Horse" meant coarse then, so horsemint really means large or coarse mint. Oswego tea got its name when the settlers around Oswego, New York, used the plant to make tea instead of buying tea from the British during the Revolution. These herbs grow in lightly wooded areas and open roadsides where they bloom from June to September. The Oswego tea is such a good-looking wildflower that it is often brought into gardens for the beauty of the red flowers and the pleasant fragrance of the leaves. Both horsemint and Oswego tea are members of the genus *Monarda*—names for Dr. Nicolas Monardes, the Spanish doctor and botanist.

tansy *Tanacetum vulgare*

This is a member of the daisy family, as its flowers show you. Tansy tea made from the leaves of the plant was a very bitter tea used to fight fevers. The tea was also held to be good for a stomachache and a cold. All in all, the settlers thought it was a very useful herb to have, and almost every herb garden had some. The plant is very long-lived, and sometimes the last remaining sign of an old homestead is the clump of tansy plants still growing where the garden used to be. It was another of those herbs used both for medicine and as food. In old recipe books you can find recipes for tansy cakes and puddings, as well as the medicinal tansy tea. Tansy has escaped from cultivation in the eastern half of North America where it blooms from July to September. The small round yellow flowers and the bitter taste of the leaves gave this herb the folk name of "bitter buttons."

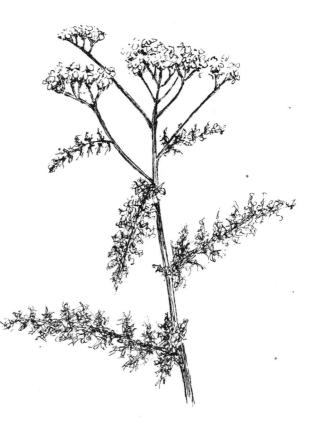

YARROW *Achillea millefolium*

Yarrow has firmer footing in Greek history than elecampane. Yarrow is called *Achillea* because Achilles was said to have stopped the bleeding of his soldiers' wounds with the fernlike green leaves of this herb. We do know that this plant was used to stop bleeding by the Greek soldiers at least as far back as 1000 B.C. Since the Trojan War is believed to have been fought around 1200 B.C., the legend may well be true. Yarrow still has the ability to stop bleeding—that is, to be a styptic. One of the common names for yarrow is "nose-bleed," because it was used to stop nose-bleeds. This plant can be found nearly all over the world. In North America you can find it in old cultivated areas and roadsides and even in city lots where the white flowers bloom from June to November.

ELECAMPANE *Inula helenium*

Elecampane was one of the first medicinal herbs to be brought to the colonies. It was part of an herb garden in Ipswich, Massachusetts, in 1640. Elecampane was used for lung infections both for people and for horses. This gave it the common name of "horseheal." Recently, the plant has been found to contain a drug that is a powerful bacteriacide. This drug is named Helenin in honor of the plant it comes from. The settlers didn't know why elecampane cured a lung infection, but they knew it did. There is a legend that *Inula helenium* got its name because long ago in ancient Greece, Helen of Troy took some of this herb with her when she was carried off. Just why, we aren't told. You can find elecampane naturalized in old cultivated areas and roadsides in the eastern half of North America where it blooms in August. The flowers look like sunflowers.

wild thyme *Thymus serphyllum*

Wild thyme, like the *Monardas,* is a member of the mint family. This herb had been used in Europe for a long time before the settlers brought it to this country. It is a plant of hills and mountains that has become at home in the eastern mountains of North America. Thyme was brought to the New World as a cure for coughs and stomachaches. Today you can go into a drugstore and find thyme in bottles on the shelf. Both thyme oil and a medicine called thymol are used in medicines as a germicide and antiseptic. You can find this low herb in dry pastures and along roadsides. The square stems and pleasant smell will help you to identify it.

mullein *Verbascum thapsus*

The mullein plant is native to Europe where it is grown
in gardens. Here we value it much less and call it a weed.
Mullein was brought to this country because the settlers
used its leaves to make a cough medicine. Mullein does
have a drug in its leaves that can be used to break up
a cough and ease a sore throat. The plant has a wide
assortment of names. It has been called Adam's flannel,
velvet plant, and blanket leaf because of its large soft
velvety leaves, and torches, hedge taper, and candlewick
because the flower stalk was dipped in fats or oils and
burned as a torch. Mullein torches were used by the
Roman armies when they invaded Europe and England.
Today we see the tall spires of mullein along the roadside
and in old fields where the yellow flowers bloom in July
and August.

cinquefoil, *Potentilla*

There are about three hundred cinquefoils in the world—one hundred here in North America. The name cinquefoil means five leaves, but not all cinquefoils have just five leaflets. In some, the leaflets are arranged like a hand, or palmately. In others, the leaflets are arranged like a feather, or pinnately. The Latin name, *Potentilla,* is used as the common name by some people. It means potent or powerful. A long time ago this herb was used as a medicine that people thought was very powerful. We enjoy the bright yellow flowers of some of the *Potentillas* now in our gardens—but we don't often realize that the plant is still used to make medicine. *Potentilla* is the source of a drug used to relieve muscle spasms. This plant grows in the sun on sandy soil in all of North America.

food

chicory *Cichorium intybus*

This pretty blue flower is closely related to lettuce. Both chicory and lettuce are members of the daisy family. The early settlers brought chicory to this country for at least two reasons. The young green leaves were eaten in salads, as they still are in Europe. (The endive that you see in grocery stores is very closely related to the wild chicory.) You can find old recipes for salads and soups using chicory or succory, as it was sometimes called. Another use was found for the roots, which were roasted and ground to make a substitute for coffee. The chicory that is added to coffee so often in the southern states comes from this flower. A third use for this herb was in making love potions. Succory was supposed to keep a lover faithful. We can find this herb growing in old fields and roadsides in the eastern half of North America and on the west coast too. Ships have brought this herb to both our shores. The pretty blue flowers bloom from July to October.

goosefoot *Chenopodium album*

The Latin name for this common plant literally means "white goosefoot." The leaves of the herb are shaped much like the feet of geese. The early settlers brought the herb to this country to use as a green vegetable, much as we use spinach. In fact, goosefoot and spinach are very closely related. The small green flowers are inconspicuous, but they produce great quantities of seed. This seed was ground into a flour for making pancakes much like buckwheat pancakes. Since the seeds are so plentiful, goosefoot spreads easily and can be found anywhere in areas of old cultivation, including cities. In fall, with the first frost, the leaves turn bright red. Once you have seen these red leaves, take a good look at the plant, and you will recognize it all the rest of the year.

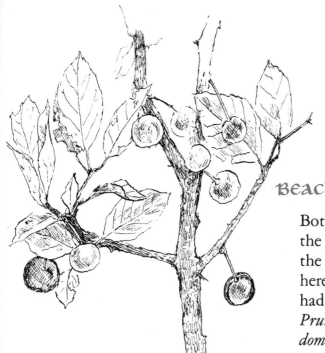

beachplum *Prunus maritima*

Both the beach plum and the sand cherry, like the raspberry and strawberry, are members of the rose family. The species the settlers found here were slightly different from those they had grown in gardens and orchards in Europe. *Prunus maritima* was smaller than the *Prunus domestica* of their homelands. The settlers used these small, wild plums in pies and jams. The plums grow on bushes in the sandy soil along the Atlantic coast.

sand cherry *Prunus besseyi*

The sand cherry is much like the beach plum of the Atlantic states. This bush grows in the central plains states. Both have white blossoms in the spring. The Indians used the fruit of both shrubs long before the first settlers arrived.

ROSE *Rosa*

The rose may not seem like food to us, but it was to the settlers. The seed pod or "hip" of the rose flower was used as food and to make jelly. We know now that these hips are very valuable because of the vitamin C they contain—something the settlers needed in the long winters of North America. Two other members of the rose family were familiar to the settlers as they explored the forests and clearings of the New World for food. Both the strawberry, *Fragaria,* and the raspberry, *Rubus,* grow wild in North America as well as in Europe.

WILD ONION *Allium*

These natives have many relatives all over the world. When the early pioneers saw the many kinds of wild onions in the open meadows of North America, they gathered them to use in the same ways they had used them in Europe. The strong-flavored kinds they called wild garlic and used to flavor foods. The mild ones they called wild onion and ate as a vegetable. The Indians used them the same way.

JERUSALEM ARTICHOKE *Helianthus tuberosu.*

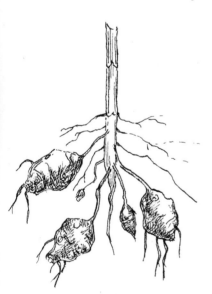

Jerusalem artichoke, like the Missouri currant, is a native of the midwestern states. This is easily one of the most poorly named plants in North America. It is not an artichoke, and it is not from Jerusalem. No one seems to know why the name artichoke was given to the plant. We do know that "Jerusalem" came from the Italian word *girasole* meaning "sun follower." The early settlers, who delighted in giving plants names from the Bible, like Solomon's seal, Eve's thread, and Adam's flannel, turned the strange-sounding *girasole* into the more familiar "Jerusalem." Actually, the Italian name is much closer to describing the plant, for it is a member of the sunflower family. The roots of the Jerusalem artichoke have tubers much like those of a potato. It is these tubers that the Indians, and later the pioneers, used as food. The plant grows five to eight feet tall on rich, moist ground. The bright yellow flowers bloom in September and October.

common sunflower *Helianthus annuus*

Like the Jerusalem artichoke, this is a member of the sunflower family. While the Jerusalem artichoke is used for its tubers and has insignificant seeds, this giant sunflower produces a great many seeds on heads that are often eight feet above the ground. *Helianthus annuus* has been greatly improved by hybridization and now produces seeds that are a major article of commerce in several European countries. The sunflower has travelled to Europe from our central states, where the plains Indians used the seed for food long before the pioneers came. It can be found in open places in central North America and occasionally in eastern North America where it has escaped from gardens or where a seed from a bird feeder has found a place to grow. The large yellow flowers bloom from July to September.

MISSOURI CURRANT *Ribes odoratum*

This is one of the plants that the Indians used to make pemmican. Pemmican was the food the Indians relied on when they went on long trips and when they went hunting and could carry little with them. Pemmican was made of cranberries pounded with fat and dried deer meat in the east. The western version was made of Missouri currants and buffalo meat. The Missouri currant is native to the central states and can be found there on dry, rocky soil. The flowers bloom in April, May, and June, and the fruits follow in late June through August.

PRAIRIE TURNIP *Psoralea esculenta*

This member of the pea family is another native of the central prairies. The starchy roots were used as food by the plains Indians, who showed the pioneers how to use them. The early pioneers, when they moved into the great central prairie from the eastern forest, needed other sources of food when the forest plants they had relied on were no longer available. The prairie turnip was one of the most important of the food plants the plains Indians gave the settlers. The purple flowers bloom in May and June.

wild potato vine *Ipomoea pandurata*

The wild potato vine is much like a very large sweet potato, but not so sweet. What it lacks in sweetness it makes up in size. The tubers can weigh as much as twenty pounds! This plant is native to North America, and was a very important food of the Indians of eastern North America. Wild potato vine is a member of the morning glory family, and has the typical morning glory flowers and vining growth. The vines may be found on dry ground where the white and pink flowers bloom from May to September.

purslane *Portulaca oleracea*

Purslane is one of the green herbs that the early settlers used a great deal as salad. It has now become a weed because of its tendency to take over any area where it can get started. *Oleracea* means oily or fat, and refers to the fat, water-filled, or succulent, leaves. It is the water in the leaves that gives this herb the ability to grow in waste places where other plants would wither. Since it is a tenacious weed of cultivation, you can find it all over North America. It is not difficult to find in cities where other plants will not grow. The many small, yellow flowers bloom from June to September, but they are hard to see because they are almost hidden by the fat, low-growing leaves.

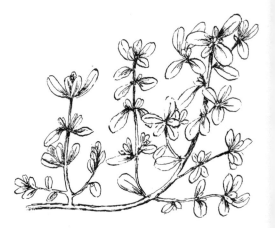

CURLY dock *Rumex crispus*

Curly dock was one of the many herbs brought to this country for use both as greens and as medicine. Since it is one of the first plants to show new green growth in the spring, it, like the dandelion, was an excellent spring tonic. It was used to make a tonic and an astringent as early as 500 B.C. Dock, or sorrel, as it is sometimes called, is still widely used in France as a green vegetable. In this country it is considered a weed. Curly dock can be found along roadsides, in places of old cultivation, and in city lots. The small, green flowers bloom from June to August.

household

BAYBERRY *Myrica cerifera*

The bayberries that grow along the eastern coast of North America have waxy berries. The berries are so waxy, in fact, that the early settlers made candles from them. When candles were one of the very few ways of lighting a room, this little plant became very important. The candles had a pleasant fragrance when they were burning. The *cerifera* of one of the Latin names means wax-bearing. The *Myricas* are bushes or small trees growing on sandy soil.

BOUNCING BET *Saponaria officinalis*

Bouncing Bet is a very lovely pink flower. The early settlers didn't bring it here for that reason alone, however. The plant has a sap or juice that when rubbed in water makes a foam. The settlers used this foam to wash their clothes. Bouncing Bet is a natural detergent. Because of this, it is also a natural poison, the same way that all detergents are poisonous. This makes it a bad plant to have in pastureland, but it is still lovely along roadsides where it blooms from June to August.

BUTTERPRINT *Abutilon theophrasti*

Butterprint is a very common plant in the midwest. The settlers called it butterprint because the seed pod makes a starlike pattern when it is pressed into something soft like butter. The early settlers, and country housewives today, used the seed pods to make pretty designs on their butter. *Abutilon* originally came from India and eastern Asia, where the fibers in the stem were used to make the backing on oriental rugs. Today we see butterprint in old fields and roadsides. This is another traveler that landed on both of our coasts and covered most of the ground in between. The yellow flowers bloom from August to October.

teasel *Dipsacus fullonum*

Teasel is a plant with a spiney seed head, much like a thistle. This plant was brought to the colonies by weavers because the seed head was used to brush up the nap on woolen material to make it soft. Even today, a teasel seed head is the only thing that will give just the right texture to fine woolens. The plants are still being grown for that reason. If you see teasels growing, you can tell that a woolen mill probably used to stand nearby. You can find teasels in old cultivated ground in the eastern half of North America. They bloom from July to September. The seed heads can be seen in brown fields in late October and November.

dyer's green weed *Genista tinctoria*

Dyer's green weed was a "weed" that was brought to this country intentionally as a source of dye. Why it was called dyer's *green* weed is a mystery, because the dye it gave was yellow. We can guess it was used for dyeing things because of the name *tinctoria,* meaning plant that tints things. You can find this plant on barren waste areas in the eastern tier of states along the Atlantic. The yellow flowers look like small sweet peas. They bloom from June to August.

63

LADY'S BEDSTRAW *Galium verum*

This wildflower has many uses. The leaves were used in colonial times to curdle milk to make cheese. A red dye was made from the roots. An astringent was made from the leaves. Finally, the entire plant, when dried and gathered into a pile, made a soft sweet-smelling bed. There is an old legend that lady's bedstraw made the first bed for the infant Jesus in the manger. According to the legend, the lady of lady's bedstraw was Mary. Lady's bedstraw was brought to this country early in its settlement. Now it can be seen in areas of old cultivation anywhere east of the Rocky Mountains. It blooms from June to September. There is another bedstraw that is very much like *Galium verum* except that it has white flowers, while *Galium verum* has yellow ones. The white-flowered kind has a wider range and may be a native.

indigo *Indigofera*

Indigo came from India—the country that gave the plant its name. It produces a blue dye that is also called indigo. Indigo was one of the first crops to be exported from the colonies to bring much-needed money for the colonists to buy the things they could not make. A young girl, Elizabeth Pinckney, first experimented with growing indigo in the colonies, and made it into an important source of money for the colonies. When she was just sixteen, she took over the management of her father's three plantations near Charleston, South Carolina. She grew indigo there, and taught other plantation owners how to raise the plant and encouraged them to grow crops of it. Soon, great cargoes of indigo were being shipped to Europe and sold. Eventually, some of that money helped to pay for the Revolutionary War. George Washington thought of Elizabeth Pinckney as one of the great patriots of Colonial America.

Plants of the Swampland

medicine

marsh mallow *Althaea officinalis*

The marsh mallow is a swamp plant that originally gave us a food you can find today in any grocery store. Marshmallows! The pioneers used marsh mallows as much for medicine as for candy. They boiled the roots with sugar to make a slippery medicine. The slipperiness of the boiled root coated and soothed sore throats. These mallows came to this country from Europe, but long before that they had come to Europe from Asia and the Middle East. They are mentioned in the Old Testament as a food plant. Marsh mallows were even used as a powerful charm against witchcraft. The marshmallows we buy in the store usually have a glycerine or gelatin base and have no connection with the ancient herb except in name. *Althaea officinalis* grows in wet land in the eastern part of North America. The pink flowers look like small hollyhock flowers. They bloom from June through August.

willow *Salix*

The bark of the willow has been used for a long time as a medicine to cure headaches and to prevent malaria. When a farmer in medieval Europe had a headache, he found a willow tree and chewed a twig of it. The twig contained an ingredient called salicylic acid. Do you know what we call salicylic acid today? Aspirin! The name *salicylic* comes from the Latin name for willow—*Salix*. Willow bark also contains a drug called salicin. Salicin contains an anti-malarial agent—that is, salicin is used as a cure for malaria. Willows are water-loving trees, and can be found near water in all parts of North America.

sweet flag *Acorus calamus*

This water-loving plant is native both to Europe and to North America. Both the Greeks and the American Indians used the root as candy and as a remedy for stomach-ache. The long iris-like leaves were used to cover the bare dirt floors of the earliest settlers' cabins. The sweet-smelling leaves made the close air of the small homes more pleasant. The settlers had learned to do this in England where leaves of the sweet flag were used to cover the floors of small homes and castles alike. You can find the strangely shaped yellow flower blooming in the swamps of eastern North America in April, May, and June.

food

cattail *Typha latifolia*

The cattail is probably the best known of all the food plants of the swamp. It provided much food for the Indians, who taught the settlers to use it as they did. The young shoots were gathered in the spring and eaten the way we eat asparagus. In some parts of Europe, these young shoots are still eaten in the spring. One of the folk names for cattail is "Cossack asparagus." Later, the flower buds can be eaten, much like corn on the cob. The Indians used the ground roots to make flour. Still later, when the flowers were in bloom, they used the plentiful pollen to add to flour to make pancakes and breads. Finally, when the seed heads were mature and starting to disperse the fluffy down, the Indians collected the down to line their sleeping bags and cradle-boards. You can find cattails growing near water all over North America, even in city parks.

WILD RICE *Zizania aquatica*

Wild rice is a swamp plant that the Indians taught the settlers to appreciate. It is not true rice, but much like it. If you go to look for it in a grocery store now, you will find it is a very special and very expensive delicacy. In several states, there are laws that say that wild rice may be harvested only by Indians, descendants of the first Indians who showed the settlers how to use the wild rice for food. Wild rice occasionally can be found in the eastern half of North America in wet, swampy land.

ARROW HEAD *Sagittaria latifolia*

The arrow head's tubers were roasted by the Indians the same way we roast potatoes. These tubers grow under water, and are difficult to find. It is said that the Indians solved the problem by using their bare toes to find the tubers. Arrow head tubers were one of the most important sources of food for Indian tribes all across North America. There were times when the Lewis and Clark expedition relied on them, too. The Indians called arrow head *wapatoo* or *katnis*. The settlers called them duck potatoes or, more elegantly, swan potatoes. These water plants grow by streams and rivers over most of North America. The pretty white flowers bloom from May to July.

CRANBERRY *Vaccinium macrocarpon*

Cranberry was one of the berries used by the eastern Indians to make pemmican. Pemmican was a combination of berries, fat, and dried meat that the Indians carried with them on long journeys. Farther west, the plains Indians used the Missouri currant. Cranberries are rich in vitamins, and were an important part of the early settlers' diet because they could be preserved for winter use. Cranberries grow only in a certain kind of bog along the east coast of North America, and only rarely farther inland to Minnesota and Illinois. The red berries appear in September and October.

INDIAN POTATO *Apios americana*

Indian potatoes or ground-nuts were one of the most important sources of food for the Indians of North America. The Pilgrims, too, depended on these Indian potatoes, along with the squash, corn, and beans of the Indian triad of food. They were mentioned as early as 1590 in a book describing Sir Walter Raleigh's explorations of the Virginias. The tubers, strung out along the roots much like the tubers of the white potato, were eaten raw or roasted. Indian potato is a vining member of the pea family. It is native to the eastern part of North America where it grows on moist soil. The purple flowers resemble sweet peas. You can find them blooming from July to September.

household

horsetail, *Equisetum arvense*

The horsetail is one of the oldest living plants. You can find fossils of *Equisetum* sometimes near the place where the plants are still growing. The early settlers used these plants to scrub pots and pans. The rough branches have a silica in them and make ideal pot scrubbers. An added advantage is that the plants grow in wet places by streams where the pioneers washed their dishes. You can use them the same way if you find horsetails on a camping trip.

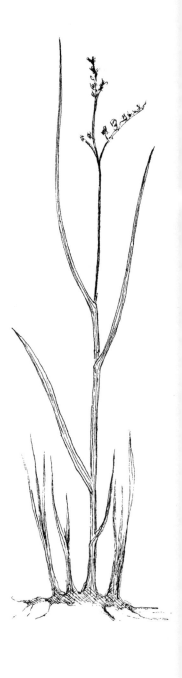

RUSHES *Juncus*

Rushes are tall grass-like plants that grow all over North America in wet and swampy places. You can tell a rush from the grasses and sedges that look like them by their round stems and the small green flowers that look like miniature lilies. Rushes are, in fact, related to the lily family, but you have to look very closely to see the resemblance. Rushes were used by the Indians and early pioneers to weave baskets and make chair seats. The pithy centers of the stems were dipped in fats to make the rush lights the settlers used for light when they had no candles.

PART III

Making your own Garden

In this book we have talked about plants growing in their native homes. You can find some of these plants in other places as well. Look at the labels on medicines sold in drugstores. You will find many of the plants listed that we have talked about. Look in grocery stores, especially on the spice racks and on the green vegetable counters. One of the best places to look for herbs is in seed catalogues. Many of the plants are for sale, either as small plants or as seeds. Most interesting of all is growing some of these plants for yourself.

Making your own garden of wild herbs is really very easy. After all, these are plants that thrive in the wild with no care at all. The most important thing for you to do is to give them a place to grow that is as much like their native homes as possible. The swamp plants won't grow for you unless you have a swamp in your backyard but many of the woodland plants will grow in a shady corner, and many more of the plants of the pastureland will thrive if given sun and a well-drained soil. In fact, many of them will come up if you just prepare the ground for them—the seeds are already there.

In the index at the back of the book, you will find lists of capital letters after some of the plants. These letters are a code to tell you which of these plants are easy to grow in your own garden.

E   Easy to grow.

S   Spreads readily. May take over.

L   Large—over two feet.

P   Pot. Can be grown on windowsill. Good for a school project.

G   Garden. Can be included in a more formal garden.

First break up the soil to a depth of about eight inches—deeper if you are going to plant large roots. Take out the rubble (the sticks and stones) and rake the soil until it is smooth.

FOR SEEDS:

Spread seeds.

Cover with fine sifting of soil.

Water. Keep soil barely damp until seeds have sprouted. Then water less often.

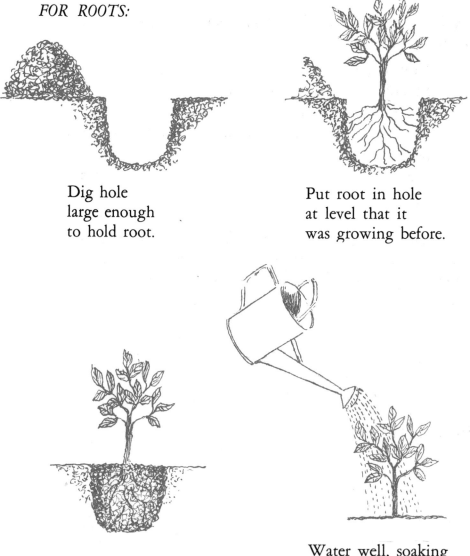

FOR ROOTS:

Dig hole
large enough
to hold root.

Put root in hole
at level that it
was growing before.

Firm soil.

Water well, soaking
ground. Leave until
it is dry again.

Collecting and Drying Plants

A good way to keep a record of the plants you have found is to collect and dry one of each kind. This is very easy to do. It is also very inexpensive.

YOU WILL NEED:

1. Some plastic bags—old bread sacks do well—and a pair of scissors to collect the plants.

2. A notebook to note when and where each plant was collected.

3. Lots of old newspapers to absorb the water while the plants are drying.

4. Two boards—plywood or Masonite do well—to form the outside of the press.

5. Books, bricks, or anything heavy that will fit on top of the press to weigh it down. If you like, you can use twine or old belts to keep the press closed and to add even pressure on the drying plants.

6. Some stiff art paper and paste for mounting the dried plants.

COLLECTING YOUR PLANTS:

1. Before you pick each plant, look carefully at the way it is growing. When you press it, you will want the dried plant to look as much as possible like a growing one.

2. Try to find examples of each plant with flowers or seeds. These help identify the plants and make your collection more interesting.

3. You will not need much of the root system, just the plant from the ground up.

4. Be sure not to crowd the plants when you put them in the plastic bags and don't leave the bags in the sun for long, or you will cook your plants!

PLANT PRESS

PRESSING YOUR PLANTS:

1. Open a section of newspaper and arrange a plant on one side of the section. Carefully close the other half of the section over on top of the plant and put the folded section on one of the boards.

2. Repeat this until all the plants are arranged, putting more newspaper between each section containing a plant to absorb more water.

3. Put the press in a warm, dry place. Put the top board on and weigh it down.

4. When each plant is dry, take it out of the press and paste it carefully on a sheet of art paper.

5. Label each plant with both Latin and common names and when and where you found it. For an even more permanent collection, you can use clear contact paper instead of paste.

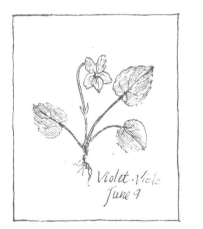

Violet - Viola
June 9

Mint - Menthe
Aug 5

Making Teas and Salads

A very easy way to enjoy these herbs of the pioneers is to make tea from the leaves. You can use the following plants to make tea:

Spearmint	*Gill-over-the-ground*
Peppermint	*Wintergreen*
Horsemint	*Sassafras*
Oswego tea	*Catnip*

1. First find the herb. Be sure you know which plant you have.

2. Pick some of the leaves. Use only the undamaged ones. You will need four or five for one cup of tea, and about a handful for a pot.

3. Wash the leaves in cool water.

4. Put the leaves in a cup or pot and pour boiling water over them.

5. Let the tea steep for three to five minutes. Vary this to your own taste.

6. Add as much sugar or honey as you like and enjoy a cup of tea the way the pioneers did.

FOR SASSAFRAS TEA:

1. Dig a few young roots.

2. Scrub them well and cut them into small pieces.

3. To make a pot of tea, boil a handful of the pieces in water until the water is a pleasant tea color.

4. Add sugar or honey. This makes good iced tea, too.

Plants you can use in salads include:

Violet leaves (young)	*Dandelion (young)*
Sour grass	*Dock (young)*
Purslane	*Chicory (young)*
Goosefoot	*Wild Thyme*
Wild Onion	

Young leaves are best because they are the most tender and have the best flavor. Because these flavors are perhaps stronger than you are used to, it might be a good idea to add these herbs to a salad of more familiar greens, at least until you learn which of the herbs you really like.

There are only two precautions: be sure you know which plant you are using and be sure that the plant has not been sprayed with insecticide or herbicide.

1. Find your herb.

2. Pick some of the young, undamaged leaves.

3. Wash them in cool water.

4. Dry and add them to your green salad.

Dyeing Cloth

You can dye material just the way the pioneers did, using many of the plants in this book. It really is very easy. Dyeing is a good fall project because many of the plant materials you will need are ready to use in the fall. A good class or club project is to dye plain white handkerchiefs each in a different color to show the colors the pioneers wore. Adding one plain handkerchief to each dye pot is also a good way to keep a record of your experiments.

Usually, natural colors are soft and subtle. If a color comes out too bright, just throw a few rusty nails into the pot. This will gray the color.

YOU WILL NEED:

1. Two to four large pots. These should be of enamel or stainless steel. At least one of them should be big enough to hold 2 to 4 gallons.
2. Some long-handled wooden spoons.
3. Some alum and some cream of tartar. Ammonium alum can be bought at the drugstore, or you can buy pickling alum at the grocery store. The grocery store will also have the cream of tartar.

4. Plastic bags or old milk cartons to collect your dye material. Include rubber gloves if you are looking for pokeberry or elderberry.
5. The plant material to make the dye.
6. The fabric you want to dye. Cotton, linen, and wool are the fabrics the pioneers used. Man-made fibers take the dye differently, but they can be interesting too. Try dyeing several different types of fabric in one dye pot so you can see these differences.
7. A stove.

PLANTS YOU CAN USE:

Pokeberry. Use the berries. Purples.

Tansy. Use the leaves. Light green.

Sassafras. Use the root as for tea, only in a stronger solution. A pretty pink-tan.

Goldenrod. Use the flower heads. Golds.

Onion. Use the dry brown skins. Yellow-browns.

Bedstraw. Use the roots. Reds.

Elderberry. Use the berries. Lavenders.

HOW TO DYE:

1. Collect your plant material. For a start, collect one-half gallon of each type of material. Empty half-gallon milk cartons are ideal for this. Your plant material will usually keep in the refrigerator for a few days before you use it.

2. On the day you choose for dyeing, you will need at least two hours' time. The dye pots won't need constant attention, but you will want to check and stir from time to time.

3. Wear old clothes!

4. Put the largest pot on the stove and fill it with water, not quite to the top.

5. Stir in 2 tablespoons of alum and 1 scant tablespoon of cream of tartar FOR EACH GALLON OF WATER. This is your mordant. Mordant makes the dye more permanent and less likely to run or fade.

6. Wet the fabric in warm tap water and put it to soak in the mordant for one hour. Keep the water just simmering and stir occasionally.

7. As soon as the fabric is in the mordant, put your plant material in the other pots and add enough water to cover it. (You can use as many pots as you have burners to keep them warm on.)

8. Simmer the plant material for one hour (one-half hour for pokeberry.)

9. At the end of the first hour, strain ALL the plant material out of the dye. You will probably have about 2 quarts of dye.

10. Take the fabric out of the mordant, wring it out slightly and put it into one of the dye pots. If the fabric is not completely covered with the dye water, add more water from the tap.

11. Simmer the fabric in the dye for one hour. Stir frequently. If your fabric is wool, don't let the water get too hot—just simmer it.

12. Rinse the fabric and spread it out to dry in a warm, dry place.

13. Let it rest for one week to set the dyes.

14. Now you have material that you dyed yourself, using the dyes of the pioneers.

Bibliography

Here is a list of other books you might like to find to read more about the plants the early settlers used.

Alexander, Taylor R., Burnett, R. Will, and Zim, Herbert S. *Botany*. New York, Golden Press, 1970.

Cavanna, Betty. *The First Book of Wild Flowers*. New York, Franklin Watts, Inc., 1961.

Coon, Nelson. *Using Wayside Plants*. Great Neck, New York, Hearthside Press, 1957.

Dana, Mrs. William Starr. *How to Know the Wildflowers*. New York, Dover, 1963.

Fox, Frances Margaret. *Flowers and Their Travels*. Indianapolis, Indiana, Bobbs-Merrill Company, 1936.

Gibbons, Euell. *Stalking the Good Life*. New York, David McKay, 1966. *Stalking the Healthful Herbs*. New York, David McKay, 1970. *Stalking the Wild Asparagus*. New York, David McKay, 1962.

Gottscho, Samuel. *The Pocket Guide to the Wildflowers*. New York, Pocket Book and Dodd Mead, 1951.

Hylander, Clarence J., Johnston, Edith Farrington. *The Macmillan Wild Flower Book*. New York, The Macmillan Company, 1954.

Lees, Carlton B. *Gardens, Plants, and Man.* Englewood Cliffs, New Jersey, Prentice-Hall, Inc., 1970.

Lehner, Ernst and Johanna. *Folklore and Odysseys of Food and Medicinal Plants.* New York, Tudor Publishing Company, 1962.

McKenny, Margaret and Johnson, Edith F. *A Book of Wild Flowers.* New York, Macmillan Company, 1939.

Northcote, Lady Rosalind. *The Book of Herb Lore.* New York, Dover, 1971.

Pistorius, Anna. *What Wildflower is It?* Chicago, Illinois, Follett Company, 1950.

Rickett, Harold William. *Wildflowers of the United States.* New York, McGraw-Hill Book Company, 1966.

Rohde, Eleanour Sinclair. *A Garden of Herbs.* New York, Dover, 1969.

Zim, Herbert S., and Martin, Alexander C. *Flowers: A Guide to Familiar American Wildflowers.* New York, Simon and Schuster, 1950.

Plants Described in this Book

About the Author

ELIZABETH SCHAEFFER was born in Urbana and received her B.A. from the University of Illinois. As a child she collected and studied local plants. This early botanical interest was later nurtured by courses she attended in field botany at the University of Illinois.

At present she teaches interior design at a community college and writes a series of articles about weeds for a local newspaper. She says that her enthusiasm for plants is continually refreshed by "digging in old herbals and just going out and sitting in a patch of weeds."

Mrs. Schaeffer lives in Iowa City, Iowa, with her husband and their two children.

About the Artist

GRAMBS MILLER was born in Peking and grew up in Tientsin, China. She has also lived in France and Mexico. An artist skilled in lithography, calligraphy, and etching, her delicate and beautiful drawings have decorated many books. One of her most recent is *Learning About Flowering Plants,* a book by Phyllis Ladyman, published by Young Scott Books.

She and her husband live in New York City. They spend their summers on Martha's Vineyard, an island off the coast of Massachusetts, where she translates her love of nature into culinary experiments such as making rose hip jam, sorrel soup, dandelion salad, and pickled jerusalem artichoke.